from SEA TO SHINING SEA
TEXAS

By Dennis Brindell Fradin

CONSULTANTS

Amy Jo Baker, Ed.D., Social Studies Curriculum Specialist,
San Antonio Independent School District

Michael R. Green, Reference Archivist, Texas State Library, Austin

Robert L. Hillerich, Ph.D., Consultant, Pinellas County Schools, Florida;
Visiting Professor, University of South Florida

CHILDRENS PRESS ®
CHICAGO

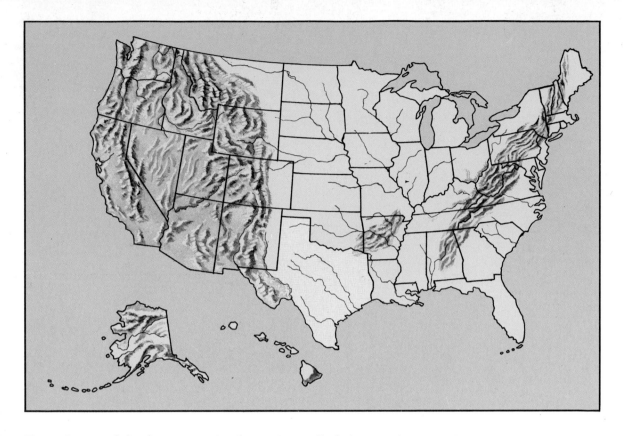

Texas is one of the four states in the region called the Southwest. The other southwestern states are Arizona, New Mexico, and Oklahoma.

For my dear uncle, Harold Brindell

Front cover picture, The Alamo at sunset; page 1, moonrise over the Chisos Mountains, Big Bend National Park; back cover, bluebonnets and phlox, Gonzales

Project Editor: Joan Downing
Design Director: Karen Kohn
Research Assistant: Judith Bloom Fradin
Typesetting: Graphic Connections, Inc.
Engraving: Liberty Photoengraving

Library of Congress Cataloging-in-Publication Data

Fradin, Dennis B.
  Texas / by Dennis Brindell Fradin.
    p.   cm. — (From sea to shining sea)
  Includes index.
  Summary: Introduces the geography, climate, history,
industries, prominent cities, and famous people of Texas.
  ISBN 0-516-03843-5
  1. Texas—Juvenile literature. [1. Texas.] I. Title.
II. Series: Fradin, Dennis B. From sea to shining sea.
F386.3.F69   1992   92-9189
976.4—dc20   CIP
                                               AC

Table of Contents

A child picking bluebonnets and Indian paintbrush

INTRODUCING THE LONE STAR STATE

Texas is the largest of the four southwestern states. In fact, of the fifty states, only Alaska is larger. Texas is famous for its great size. Texas has had a colorful history. At first, Spain, and then Mexico, ruled Texas. In 1836, the Texans fought for and won their independence. Two of America's greatest western heroes helped in that war. They were Sam Houston and Davy Crockett. For almost ten years, Texas stood alone. It was an independent republic. A lone star was on its flag. Today, Texas is called the "Lone Star State."

Texas became famous for its cowboys, lawmen, and outlaws. Today, the state is known for its farms and industries. Texas leads the country in producing oil and natural gas. It is still the top state for raising beef cattle.

Texas is famous for many other things. Where is the famous building called the Alamo? Where were Presidents Dwight D. Eisenhower and Lyndon B.

Johnson born? Where are the Johnson Space Center and the Houston Astrodome? The answer to all these questions is: Texas!

Overleaf: The Rio Grande and the Chisos Mountains at sunrise, Big Bend National Park

A picture map of Texas

A Texas-sized State

A Texas-sized State

To show that something is big, the word Texas-sized is used. A "Texas-sized ranch" covers much land. Someone with a "Texas-sized appetite" is very hungry. Texas covers 266,807 square miles. It is the second-largest state.

Texas is one of the four states in the region called the Southwest. Four other states border Texas. Louisiana and Arkansas lie to the east. Oklahoma is to the north. New Mexico is to the west. Another country—Mexico—is south and southwest of Texas. The Gulf of Mexico is to the southeast.

Texas has a wide variety of scenery. The state has hills, mountains, and canyons. It has grasslands, deserts, and wetlands. Texas also has seacoast and islands.

Far western Texas has the most mountains. They are part of the Rocky Mountains. The highest peak in Texas is Guadalupe Peak. This peak stands 8,751 feet high.

The rest of Texas consists of plains. These level lands are broken in places by hills and mountains. The state's lowest points are on the Gulf Coastal

Seashells on the beach at Padre Island

Plain. This lies along the Gulf of Mexico. There Texas is at sea level. Off the coast are islands.

Rivers, Plants, and Animals

Texas has three very famous rivers. The Rio Grande forms the Texas-Mexico border. The Red River forms most of the Texas-Oklahoma border. The Pecos flows through West Texas. Other Texas rivers include the Brazos, Colorado, Sabine, and Trinity.

The pecan is the Texas state tree. Other important trees are gums, oaks, and pines. Each

Rio grande is Spanish, meaning "large river."

Left: The Rio Grande at Big Hill, Texas

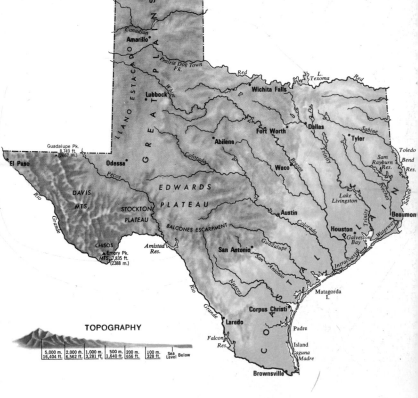

TOPOGRAPHY

| 5,000 m. 16,404 ft. | 2,000 m. 6,562 ft. | 1,000 m. 3,281 ft. | 500 m. 1,640 ft. | 200 m. 656 ft. | 100 m. 328 ft. | Sea Level | Below |

Pitcher plants are among the 4,000 kinds of wildflowers that grow in Texas.

spring, Texas is bright with wildflowers. More than 4,000 different kinds of wildflowers grow there. The bluebonnet is the state flower.

Three or four million deer roam through Texas. The state also has thousands of pronghorn antelopes. Alligators live in the wetlands. Armadillos can be found throughout the state. These animals have bony plates that look like armor. Bobcats, mountain lions, and coyotes also live in Texas.

CLIMATE

Texas has a generally warm climate. Summer temperatures in southern Texas often reach 100 degrees Fahrenheit. Winter temperatures there top 50 degrees Fahrenheit on most days. However, winter days can get very cold in West and North Texas. Amarillo, in North Texas, gets snow every year. East Texas gets about 30 inches more rain each year than West Texas.

Texas suffers from floods, droughts, tornadoes, and hurricanes. Floods in late 1991 and early 1992 killed at least ten Texans. At other times, Texas has long dry spells. These dry periods are called droughts. There is little rain. Crops and grasses die. Topsoil turns to dust and blows away.

Texas also gets hit by strong windstorms. The state is in "Tornado Alley." About one hundred tornadoes strike Texas each year. No other state gets as many. On April 10, 1979, a tornado with three funnels hit Wichita Falls. It killed forty-six people.

Hurricanes sometimes slam into the Texas coast. In 1900, one of these huge windstorms hit Galveston. More than seventy thousand people were killed. This was the worst natural disaster in American history.

The Chisos Mountains at Big Bend National Park

*From Ancient Times
Until Today*

From Ancient Times Until Today

Millions of years ago, Texas was home to many interesting animals. Dinosaurs roamed the land. Saber-toothed cats prowled through Texas. Small horses also lived in Texas. They were only 15 inches tall. There were also camels, mammoths, and mastodons.

Opposite: Mission Concepcion, San Antonio

Mammoths and mastodons were relatives of modern-day elephants.

American Indians

The first people arrived in Texas about 12,000 years ago. Those ancient Indians hunted the mammoths and mastodons. Some of the Indians lived in caves. They drew pictures on the caves' walls.

By the year A.D. 1500, many Indian groups lived in Texas. The Caddos were a united group of about twenty-five smaller Indian groups. They lived

An artist's depiction of an East Texas Caddo farming community

The Comanches were among the American Indian groups that were living in Texas before the arrival of the Spanish explorers.

in East Texas. The Caddos called each other *tejas,* or "friends." Later, Spaniards changed this slightly to *texas.* Other Texas Indian groups included the Tonkawas, Comanches, Jumanos, and Karankawas.

SPANISH EXPLORERS

Spain conquered Mexico and other New World lands during the 1500s. Spaniard Alonso Álvarez de Piñeda was the first known explorer in Texas. He explored the Texas coast in 1519.

Nine years later, a Spanish ship was wrecked along the Texas coast. Three Spaniards and a black slave named Estevánico survived. The four men traveled through Texas. Indians told them some tall tales. Somewhere in the area, said the Indians, were cities made of gold. Other Spaniards came to Texas in search of the golden cities. Spain claimed Texas based on those explorations.

SPAIN RULES TEXAS

For many years, Spain did little about settling Texas. Then, in 1682, Spanish priests founded two missions at present-day El Paso. The priests taught the Indians about Christianity at these settlements.

France also wanted Texas. In 1685, French explorer René-Robert Cavelier, Sieur de La Salle, began a colony. It was on the Texas coast. This colony didn't last long. La Salle's men died from diseases or Indian attacks. But the French colony spurred the Spaniards to settle Texas.

Mission San Jose, in San Antonio, was established in 1720.

In 1690, the Spaniards built a mission in East Texas. Over the next sixty years, they built twenty more Texas missions. Near some of the missions, the Spaniards built *presidios* (forts). These missions and forts were the start of several Texas cities. Mission San Antonio de Valero was founded in 1718. This mission became known as the Alamo. It was the start of the city of San Antonio.

Spanish settlers moved to Texas during the 1700s. They came mainly from Mexico. Many of these settlers started cattle ranches. They brought long-horned cattle from Mexico. Cowboys, called *vaqueros* in Spanish, tended the cattle. Yet, by 1800, Texas had only 4,000 Spanish settlers. That wasn't enough people to rule so huge a region.

THE AMERICANS ARRIVE

The United States gained its independence from England in 1783. This new country was along the

Stephen Austin (above) is called the "Father of Texas."

The United States had sent more people to Texas in 15 years than Spain and Mexico had in 150 years.

Atlantic Coast. But the Americans kept pushing westward. By the early 1800s, their eyes were on Texas.

Moses Austin came to San Antonio in 1820. He asked the Spanish governor to let him start an American colony. Permission was granted in early 1821. Two events of that year could have ended this plan. Moses Austin died, and Mexico broke free of Spain. Then, Texas belonged to Mexico.

Stephen Austin took charge of his father's plan. He brought 300 families into Texas in 1821. They were farmers. They settled along the Brazos River near present-day Houston. Between 1821 and 1831, Stephen Austin brought about 6,000 Americans into Texas.

Other people also got grants from Mexico to start colonies. Thousands of other Americans came to Texas. Most of the newcomers were from the southern states. Many southerners brought slaves with them. They used the slaves to plant cotton.

In 1834, an army general named Santa Anna seized control of Mexico's government. Santa Anna began taking away the Texans' rights. By that time, Texas had perhaps 30,000 settlers. Most Texans were from the United States. They didn't want to be part of Mexico.

THE TEXAS WAR OF INDEPENDENCE

War between Texas and Mexico began on October 2, 1835. That day, Texas farmers defeated Mexican forces at Gonzales, near San Antonio. Soon, the Texans also captured Goliad and San Antonio.

In Mexico, Santa Anna raised an army to fight the rebels. The men marched to San Antonio. There, some Texans had taken refuge in the Alamo.

Santa Anna's army began attacking the Alamo on February 23, 1836. Under William Travis, their leader, the rebels fired back. Davy Crockett was at the Alamo. So was Jim Bowie. But there were only 189 rebels. Against them were more than 5,000

Mexican general Antonio Lopez de Santa Anna (above, on the left) led the attack against the defenders of the Alamo (below).

The Battle of San Jacinto (above) was fought near present-day Houston.

men. The rebels could have tried to escape from the Alamo. Yet, they chose to fight to the death.

Day after day, the two sides exchanged gunfire. Then, early on March 6, Santa Anna's men rushed the Alamo. They climbed over the walls into the grounds. There was a great battle. By eight in the morning, all the Texas troops were dead. Six hundred Mexican soldiers also were dead.

Texas leaders had met during the fight at the Alamo. On March 2, 1836, they issued the Texas Declaration of Independence. It said that Texas was free of Mexico. Sam Houston was chosen to lead the Texas army.

Santa Anna showed the rebels no mercy. On March 27, at Goliad, he ordered 350 Texans shot to death. They were soldiers who were being held prisoner. This further angered the Texans. More than ever they wanted to win their freedom.

Sam Houston awaited his chance to strike. It came on April 21, 1836, along the San Jacinto River. "Remember the Alamo! Remember Goliad!" the Texans shouted as they fought. Santa Anna's forces were crushed at the Battle of San Jacinto. That victory won independence for Texas.

A COUNTRY CALLED TEXAS

Texas was free of Mexico. But Texas wasn't part of the United States. It was a country of its own called the Republic of Texas. Sam Houston became the republic's first president in late 1836. The republic issued its own paper money. It had its own flag.

Sam Houston (above) led the Texans in the Battle of San Jacinto.

Below: A sample of the paper money issued by the Republic of Texas

By 1848, 42,000 slaves lived in Texas.

That is now the Texas state flag. One star appeared on the Texas flag and money. That's why Texas was called the "Lone Star Republic."

Texas remained a country for nearly ten years. New towns were founded. Houston and Galveston were begun in 1836. Austin was founded in 1839. Dallas was founded in 1841. During those years, most Texans were farmers or ranchers.

Sam Houston wanted Texas to join the United States. Most Texans agreed. The United States annexed Texas in March 1845. On December 29, 1845, Texas became the twenty-eighth state.

Mexico and the United States argued over the Texas-Mexico border. They also argued over owner-ship of California. War broke out in 1846. The United States won the Mexican War in 1848. The Rio Grande was then recognized as the Texas-Mexico border. The United States also got California and land in the southwest.

THE CIVIL WAR

Texas and the other southern states allowed slavery. By 1848, 42,000 of the 158,000 Texans were black slaves. Many of the Texas slaves grew cotton on large farms.

Slavery had been outlawed in the northern states. Southerners feared that Abraham Lincoln would end slavery in the South. Lincoln was elected president in November 1860. In December, the southern states began to secede from (leave) the Union. Texas left the Union in March 1861. Eleven southern states formed the Confederate States of America.

Costumed marchers took part in this historic parade in Granbury.

In April 1861, the Confederate states (the South) and the Union (the North) began fighting. This was the start of the Civil War (1861-1865). Fifty thousand Texans joined the Confederate army. About 2,000 joined the Union army.

Texas was the site of the war's last battle. This was the Battle of Palmito Hill. It was fought near Brownsville on May 13, 1865. The Confederates won the Battle of Palmito Hill. But the Union had won the war a month earlier! That news had not reached the soldiers at Palmito Hill. On June 19, 1865, Union officials freed all slaves in Texas.

TRAIL DRIVES AND RAILROADS

Texas farms were in bad shape after the Civil War. There were no slaves to take care of the cotton crop. Texans turned to cattle ranching more than ever. Trails were blazed between Texas and points northward. Cowboys drove the cattle north to market along these trails. The big trail drives lasted from 1866 to the 1880s.

The building of railroads ended the trail drive period. In the 1880s, railroads started taking cattle to northern markets. The railroads also brought more settlers to Texas.

The settlers pushed the Indians out of Texas. The Comanches and other West Texas Indians fought back. But they couldn't defeat the United States soldiers and settlers. By the 1880s, most Texas Indians were on reservations in Oklahoma.

Branding on the L. S. Ranch, 1908

OIL, WORLD WARS, AND DEPRESSION

Oil had first been found in Texas in 1866. But the first huge oil discovery came in 1901. That year, Anthony Lucas was drilling at Spindletop Hill near Beaumont. On January 10, oil shot out of the ground. It spurted 200 feet into the sky. This great discovery is known as the Spindletop gusher.

Hundreds of oil workers soon came to Texas. Many more oil finds were made. Texas became the leading oil-producing state in 1928. It still is today.

The United States entered World War I (1914-1918) in 1917. More than 200,000 Texans served.

During the war, James E. "Pa" Ferguson was governor. Ferguson worked to help small farmers and country schools. Miriam A. "Ma" Ferguson was his wife. She governed Texas from 1925 to 1927. She served again from 1933 to 1935. Ferguson was the nation's second woman governor. She helped crush the power of the Ku Klux Klan in Texas. This hate group had terrorized black Texans for years. Ferguson also helped poor Texans survive the Great Depression (1929-1939).

World War II (1939-1945) helped end the depression. Texans got jobs making airplanes and ships for the war. Over half the oil for the war came

Miriam "Ma" Ferguson (below) was the nation's second woman governor. Nellie Tayloe Ross of Wyoming had become the nation's first woman governor earlier that year.

from Texas. About 750,000 Texans served in the war. One of them was Audie Murphy of Farmersville. He won more medals than any other American soldier. In one battle, Murphy held off 250 enemy soldiers by himself. Texas native General Dwight D. Eisenhower was supreme commander of the European forces during the war.

TEXAS AND THE PRESIDENCY

Texas has had close ties to the office of president since World War II. Dwight D. "Ike" Eisenhower became the thirty-fourth president in 1953. He served until 1961. In that year, John F. Kennedy of Massachusetts became president. Lyndon B. Johnson of Texas was Kennedy's vice-president.

On November 22, 1963, President Kennedy was visiting Dallas. Crowds cheered as the car carrying Kennedy passed. Texas governor John Connally was riding with him. Johnson was in another car. Suddenly, shots rang out. Kennedy and Connally were both hit. Connally lived. The president died minutes later. Vice-president Lyndon B. Johnson then became the thirty-sixth president.

President Johnson worked to give blacks their civil rights. In the 1960s, black southerners were

Texan Audie Murphy was a World War II hero.

Lyndon B. Johnson was president from 1963 to 1969.

24

still kept from voting. Black children could not attend the same schools as white children. During Johnson's presidency, laws that kept blacks from voting were ended. Texas and other southern states integrated many schools. Black children and white children began attending the same schools.

President Johnson continued America's work in space. The Manned Spacecraft Center opened in Houston in 1964. In July 1969, it directed the most famous space flight in history. That was the first landing of people on the moon. The center was later renamed the Johnson Space Center.

NASA rockets are exhibited at the Johnson Space Center in Houston.

George Bush became the forty-first president in 1989. Bush was born in Massachusetts. However, the Lone Star State claims him, too. Bush ran oil companies in Texas in the 1950s and 1960s. He also served Texas as a member of Congress (1967-1971).

POPULATION BOOM AND TEXAS-SIZED PROBLEMS

Texas has enjoyed a population boom in recent years. Between 1950 and 1990, the population doubled. The number of Texans rose from 7.7 million to 16.9 million.

Many people came to Texas seeking jobs. The oil business was doing well. Many homes and offices were built. But lately, Texas has had a big shortage of jobs. During the 1980s, oil and natural gas prices dropped. Many new buildings stood empty. Other Texas industries also slumped. By 1993, Texas had a very high jobless rate.

The shortage of jobs has caused much poverty in Texas. By the early 1990s, one-fourth of Texas's children lived in poverty. The strip along the Mexican border is a very poor area.

Texas also must improve its schools. One-sixth of all adult Texans cannot read or write. Few other states have an illiteracy rate that high.

People who are illiterate cannot read or write.

Pollution is another problem. The Rio Grande and the Colorado River are filthy in places. Oil spills have occurred along the Gulf Coast. Chemical companies have released harmful matter into the air and water.

Ann Richards was elected governor in 1990. She was the state's second woman governor. Governor Richards served until 1994. The new governor, George W. Bush, and other Texans are working to tackle the state's problems.

In 1992, Texas began a lottery. Money from it will help improve the Lone Star State.

Ann Richards celebrated her victory on the night she won the election for governor of Texas.

Overleaf: A young cowgirl on the range near Bandera

Texans and
Their
Work

TEXANS AND THEIR WORK

The United States Census counted 16,986,510 Texans in 1990. Only California and New York have more people. Texas has six of the thirty largest United States cities. That's more than any other state. The six cities are Houston, Dallas, San Antonio, El Paso, Austin, and Fort Worth.

Texans are an interesting blend of people. Three-fourths of them are white. One-eighth of all Texans are black. Texas is home to 4.3 million Hispanics. That's more than any state except California. These people are of Spanish-speaking background. Almost 333,000 Texans are of Asian origin. About 65,000 are American Indians.

This mix of people spices up life in Texas. It certainly spices up the food. Mexican dishes such as chili, tacos, and burritos are popular in Texas. Chili is the state food.

Texas has holidays to honor its various people. January 19 is Confederate Heroes Day in Texas. This day honors those who fought in the Civil War. June 19 is Emancipation Day. This holiday celebrates the freeing of Texas slaves in 1865. Many

Texas is home to people of many different racial and ethnic backgrounds.

A cowgirl near Laredo

Texas cities hold Mexican-style festivals called *fiestas.*

Texas is also known for its rodeos. At these events, cowboys and cowgirls show their skills. They ride bucking broncos. They also rope cows.

HOW THEY EARN THEIR LIVING

Texas is a top manufacturing, mining, farming, and fishing state. If Texas were a country, it would be one of the world's richest.

A million Texans make products. Texas leads the country at making chemicals. Texas also leads the country at refining oil and at making plastics. It is among the top five producers of foods. Texas is also a leading maker of airplanes and paints.

Another 1.7 million Texans work at selling goods. About 1.6 million are service workers. These people include lawyers, hotel workers, nurses, and doctors. More than a million Texans work for the government. Many work at the army and air force bases.

Mining employs about 250,000 Texans. The state leads the country at producing oil and natural gas. Cars use gasoline made from Texas oil. Many homes around the country are heated by natural gas

Alaska is almost tied with Texas as the leading oil-producing state.

30

from Texas. The Lone Star State is the country's top helium producer. This light gas helps get rockets into space. It also keeps scientific balloons in the air.

Texas has about 185,000 farms and ranches. This is by far the most of any state. Texas leads the country at raising beef cattle. Texas is also the leader at raising horses and sheep. Texas also leads the states at growing cotton and watermelons. Texas is among the top growers of rice, peanuts, pecans, and hay. Grapefruit, oranges, and cucumbers are other leading crops. Other Texas farm products include milk, sugar beets, tomatoes, and lettuce.

The Gulf of Mexico helps make Texas a top fishing state. It is a leading state for catching shrimp. Crabs and oysters are other Texas shellfish. Drum, flounder, and red snapper are also caught off the Texas coast.

A Texas oil worker on an oil rig in the Gulf of Mexico

There are fifteen million beef cattle on Texas ranches.

A Trip Through
the Lone Star State

A Trip Through the Lone Star State

Pages 32-33: Cowboys rounding up cattle in West Texas

Texas offers much to see and do. There is something for everyone. Big cities and small towns alike tell Texas's history. Visitors enjoy the state's beaches, plains, and mountains. They also find that Texans tend to be friendly. Texans live up to the state's motto: "Friendship."

The Texas Panhandle

The Panhandle is a good place to begin a trip through Texas. This part of the state is shaped like a pan's handle. It makes up northwest Texas.

The Panhandle produces much of the country's oil and natural gas. It is also the world's leading helium-producing area. The Helium Monument in Amarillo reminds visitors of this.

Amarillo is the Panhandle's biggest city. The city was begun in 1887. It grew along the railroad

Quarter horses (below) are raised on ranches in the Amarillo area. The quarter horse was the first kind of horse bred in the United States.

The Red River, in Palo Duro Canyon State Park

tracks. Amarillo is in a cattle-raising area. The city is a meat-packing center. Quarter horses are raised on area ranches. These sure-footed, strong horses have long been a favorite with cowboys.

Palo Duro Canyon State Park is outside Amarillo. The canyon is 1,200 feet deep. On summer nights, the musical show *Texas* is performed at the canyon's outdoor theater. *Texas* tells the story of the people who settled the Panhandle.

South of Amarillo is Hereford. It was named for the area's herds of Hereford cattle. The National Cowgirl Hall of Fame is in Hereford. It honors women's role in ranching and in settling the West. Each summer, Hereford hosts a rodeo for women and girls.

The Panhandle also has two wildlife refuges. Buffalo Lake National Wildlife Refuge is near Hereford. Huge numbers of ducks and geese winter there. To the south is Muleshoe National Wildlife Refuge. It is near the town of Muleshoe. A large population of sandhill cranes nests there.

WEST TEXAS

Guadalupe Peak (below) is the highest point in Texas.

Lubbock is south of Amarillo. Founded in 1890-91, it was headquarters for buffalo hunters. Today, it is the center of the country's biggest cotton-growing region. Ranching Heritage Center is in Lubbock. Thirty old ranch buildings have been moved there. They provide a good picture of pioneer ranch life.

Midland and Odessa are south of Lubbock. These two cities are in another big oil-producing region. They are home to many oil companies and oil workers. The Odessa Meteor Crater is outside Odessa. A meteorite crashed there more than 20,000 years ago.

Guadalupe Mountains National Park is between Odessa and El Paso. The park is a place of deep canyons and tall mountain peaks. Guadalupe Peak, the state's highest point, is there. So is the striking peak called El Capitan.

El Paso is in the state's far western corner. It is separated from Juarez, Mexico, by the Rio Grande. This region was the first part of Texas settled by Europeans. The state's oldest Spanish mission is in El Paso. It is called Ysleta Mission. It was built in 1682 for the Tigua Indians. Today, the Tiguas have a reservation in El Paso.

El Paso is a large clothes-making center. Many oil refineries and food plants are also found there. Fort Bliss, a famous army post, is near the city.

Downriver from El Paso is Big Bend National Park. The Rio Grande makes a big bend there. Long ago, dinosaurs roamed this area of mountains,

Ysleta Mission, in El Paso

More kinds of birds have been seen at Big Bend (below) than at any other United States national park.

canyons, and deserts. Today, deer, coyotes, and mountain lions live in the park.

The Pecos River is another important river in West Texas. East of the park it flows into the Rio Grande.

AUSTIN AND SAN ANTONIO

Austin, the state capital, is not far from the center of Texas. It was founded in 1839. Texas lawmakers meet at the state capitol in Austin. This building looks much like the United States Capitol in Washington, D.C. Statues of Stephen Austin and

Sam Houston are inside the state capitol. They were made by Elisabet Ney. She was a German sculptor. In 1892, Ney moved to Austin. The Elisabet Ney Museum in Austin has many examples of her work.

The University of Texas at Austin is one of America's largest schools. The Texas Memorial Museum is at the university. Its displays tell Texas's story from the time of the dinosaurs.

West of Austin is Stonewall. President Lyndon Johnson was born and died there. He grew up in nearby Johnson City. Visitors can tour his Stonewall birthplace and Johnson City boyhood home.

Southwest of Austin is San Antonio. This is Texas's third-largest city. San Antonio is called the "Alamo City." The famous mission where Texans fought for independence can be visited. San Antonio also has four other Spanish missions. Mission San Jose is called "Queen of Missions." It gives the best idea of life at a mission.

About 60 percent of San Antonio's people have a Spanish-speaking background. Most of these people trace their roots to Mexico. San Antonio's Spanish history has been restored in La Villita. It shows how San Antonio looked 250 years ago.

Today, San Antonio is famous for its twenty-one-block River Walk. Shops, hotels, and cafes line

These Hispanic girls performing in San Antonio are part of a folkloric dance group.

39

A whale performs at Sea World of Texas.

Corpus Christi *is Latin, meaning "Body of Christ."*

the San Antonio River. People ride paddleboats or water taxis.

San Antonio is also home to Sea World of Texas. Whales, dolphins, and other sea animals can be seen there. The city has a pro basketball team. It's called the San Antonio Spurs.

FAR SOUTHERN BORDER AND GULF COAST

Laredo is southwest of San Antonio. It lies on the Rio Grande. A bridge over the Rio Grande connects Laredo and Mexico. Laredo has a large Mexican-American population.

Brownsville is the state's southernmost city. It also is on the Rio Grande. East of Brownsville is Palmito Hill Battlefield. The last Civil War battle was fought on this spot. Today, shipping and deep-sea fishing are important in Brownsville.

The Texas coast stretches for nearly 400 miles. This region is called the Gulf Coast. It lies along the Gulf of Mexico. Corpus Christi is on the Gulf Coast. The city has one of the country's busiest ports.

Several Gulf Coast islands are linked to the Texas mainland by bridges. Padre Island is across from Corpus Christi.

Galveston Island is north of Corpus Christi. The city of Galveston is on this island. It is a cotton-shipping center. Its beaches make Galveston a popular tourist spot. Today, a seawall protects Galveston from hurricanes. In 1900, there was nothing to help Galveston. The Galveston County Museum has displays on the famous hurricane of 1900.

Houston is northwest of Galveston. The city was begun in 1836. It is now Texas's biggest city. Oil discoveries during the early 1900s helped Houston grow. The Houston region is America's leading center for refining oil. It is also a major chemical-making area.

A train depot scene of the 1930s has been re-created at Galveston's Railroad Museum.

Corpus Christi

The Johnson Space Center is southeast of Houston. The center directs many space projects. Some of them have launched Americans into space. Astronauts are also trained there.

The Astrodome is another highlight of Houston. The Houston Astros play baseball in the Astrodome. The Houston Oilers play football there. Houston also has a pro basketball team, the Rockets.

San Jacinto Battleground State Historic Park is near Houston. Sam Houston and his men won Texas's independence there in 1836.

The Houston Ship Channel passes near the San Jacinto Monument. This channel connects Houston

The Visitor Center at the Johnson Space Center (below) has many space-equipment exhibits.

to the Gulf of Mexico. Houston's port is the country's third busiest.

EAST AND NORTH TEXAS

Nacogdoches is in East Texas. It is north of Beaumont. It is one of Texas's oldest towns. It grew from a Spanish mission founded in 1716. Texas's first newspaper was published in Nacogdoches in 1813. Today, Nacogdoches is the center of Texas's pine-tree country.

Texarkana is at the state's northeastern corner. Part of Texarkana is in Texas. Another part is in Arkansas. State Line Avenue separates the two states. Texarkana's factories make tires, furniture, and food. Nearby lakes and rivers are good for fishing.

Dallas is west of Texarkana. It was founded in 1841. The city's nickname is "Big D." Oil found in the region in the 1930s helped Dallas grow. Today, "Big D" is the state's second-largest city. It is a center for banking and insurance companies. It is also the country's third-largest fashion center.

Dallas was once a big cotton market. That's why the stadium in Fair Park is called the Cotton Bowl. Each New Year's Day a famous college football game is played there.

The NCNB Center, in Houston

43

The 1978 Super Bowl champion Dallas Cowboys carry coach Tom Landry off the field.

It is called Six Flags Over Texas because Texas has been under six flags. They are the flags of France, Spain, Mexico, the Republic of Texas, the Confederate States of America, and the United States.

The John F. Kennedy Memorial Plaza has a monument to the late president. It stands 200 yards from where Kennedy was shot. Dallas's Sixth Floor Museum has displays about the assassination.

Dallas has pro football and basketball teams. The Mavericks play basketball in Dallas. The Cowboys play football in Irving, just west of Dallas.

West of Dallas is Fort Worth. It began as an army post in 1849. In its early years, Fort Worth was a famous cowboy town. Today, airplane and oil companies are important in Fort Worth. The cattle business remains strong.

Fort Worth has some fine museums. One is the Amon Carter Museum of Western Art. It has works by Frederic Remington and other western artists. The Cattleman's Museum tells the story of cattle ranching in the Southwest.

Between Dallas and Fort Worth is Arlington. Six Flags Over Texas is in Arlington. It is a famous amusement park. The Texas Rangers play pro baseball at The Ballpark at Arlington.

Wichita Falls is in North Texas. An oil boom in the early 1900s helped Wichita Falls grow. Today, there are about 150 manufacturing companies in the city. Their products include plate glass, engines, and oil-drilling machines.

Vernon is northwest of Wichita Falls. It lies near the Red River. Vernon is a good place to end a Texas trip. The country's largest ranch is between Vernon and Wichita Falls. It is the Waggoner Ranch. The ranch takes up about 850 square miles.

The Dallas skyline at dusk

The Red River Valley Museum in Vernon has displays on Indians and pioneers. It also has sculptures by Electra Waggoner Biggs. She was a member of the Waggoner ranching family.

Vernon is a special town. A tornado destroyed part of Vernon in 1979. Eleven people were killed. Many others were hurt. Rebuilding Vernon helped bring its people together.

A Gallery of
Famous
Texans

A GALLERY OF FAMOUS TEXANS

Frontiersman Davy Crockett

Opposite: A painting of General Dwight David Eisenhower, who became president of the United States in 1953

Many Texans have become world famous. They include baseball stars, singers, actors, and authors. Government leaders, including two presidents, were born in Texas.

David "Davy" Crockett (1786-1836) was born in Tennessee. He became a famous bear hunter, storyteller, and Tennessee lawmaker. Crockett moved to Texas in 1835. There, he fought for Texas's independence. In 1836, he was killed defending the Alamo. Movies, television shows, and songs have been created about him.

Samuel "Sam" Houston (1793-1863) settled in Texas in 1835. He led the army that freed the region from Mexico. Houston then served as the Republic of Texas's first president. When Texas became a state, he served as a U.S. senator from Texas. Later, he was elected governor of Texas.

Quanah Parker (1845-1911) was born near what is now Lubbock. In 1867, he became a Comanche chief. Parker led attacks on frontier settlements. In 1874, his people were defeated. The Comanches were forced to live on reservations in

Oklahoma. There, Parker founded Indian schools. He also taught his people modern ways to farm.

John Nance Garner (1868-1967) was born in Red River County. He was Franklin D. Roosevelt's vice-president (1933-1941). Garner then went back to his Texas ranch. He lived to be ninety-nine.

Dwight D. Eisenhower (1890-1969) was born in Denison. He became a very famous general. During World War II, he led the Allied army in Europe. In 1952, he was elected president of the United States. He served until 1961.

Lyndon B. Johnson (1908-1973) was born near Stonewall. He was a congressman and then a

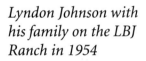

Lyndon Johnson with his family on the LBJ Ranch in 1954

senator from Texas. In 1960, he became John F. Kennedy's vice-president. When Kennedy was assassinated in 1963, Johnson became president.

Oveta Culp Hobby (1904-1995) was born in Killeen. She founded the Women's Army Corps (WAC). In 1953, Hobby became the first secretary of health, education, and welfare.

Civil-rights leader **James Farmer** was born in Marshall in 1920. In 1942, he helped found the Congress of Racial Equality (CORE). This group works for equal rights for black people.

Lawyer and politician Barbara Jordan

Politician Henry Cisneros

Barbara Jordan was born in Houston in 1936. In 1967, she became the first black woman to serve in the Texas state Senate. In 1972, she became the first southern black woman to serve in the U.S. House of Representatives.

Henry Cisneros was born in San Antonio in 1947. He became mayor of San Antonio from 1981-1989. He was the first Hispanic-American mayor of a large U.S. city. In 1993, he became the U.S. Secretary of Housing and Urban Development.

Ann Richards was born near Waco in 1993. She was governor of Texas from 1990-1994.

Author **Katherine Anne Porter** (1890-1980) was born in Indian Creek. She wrote many great

Choreographer and dancer Alvin Ailey

Actor Steve Martin

short stories. She received a Pulitzer Prize in 1966. Her popular novel *Ship of Fools* was made into a movie. Author **J. Frank Dobie** (1888-1964) was born in Live Oak County. Dobie wrote many books about Texas cowboys and pioneers.

Composer **Scott Joplin** (1868-1917) was born in Texarkana. He was known as the "King of Ragtime." This is a lively kind of piano music. Dancer **Alvin Ailey** (1931-1989) was born in Rogers. He composed dances and had his own dance company.

Movie star **Joan Crawford** (1908-1977) was born in San Antonio. Crawford won the Academy Award for best actress in 1945. Stage actress **Mary Martin** (1931-1990) was born in Weatherford. One of her best-loved roles was as Peter Pan. Actor **Steve Martin** was born in Waco in 1945.

Gene Autry was born in Tioga in 1907. He played a singing cowboy in western movies. Autry also wrote many songs. Today, he owns the California Angels baseball team. Country-and-western singer **Willie Nelson** was born in Waco in 1933.

Denton Cooley was born in Houston in 1920. He became a heart surgeon. In 1969, he placed the first artificial heart in a patient.

Many great athletes have been Texans. **Jack Johnson** (1878-1946) was born in Galveston. He became the first black heavyweight boxing champion. Golfer **Ben Hogan** was born in Dublin, Texas, in 1912. In 1949, Hogan was badly hurt in a car crash. People thought he might never walk again. Yet, he went on to win six more titles. Golf star **Lee Trevino** was born in Dallas in 1939.

Famed race-car driver **A. J. Foyt** was born in Houston in 1935. **Johnny Rutherford** is another race-car champion. He was born in Fort Worth in

Mary Martin (right) in her role as Peter Pan

Race-car driver A. J. Foyt

1938. Jockey **Willie Shoemaker** was born in Fabens in 1931. He won 8,833 horse races, more than any other jockey. A tragic accident in 1993 left him a quadriplegic.

One of the best woman athletes in history was born in Port Arthur. Her name was **Mildred "Babe" Didrikson Zaharias** (1914-1956). Zaharias won two gold medals in the 1932 Olympics. One was for throwing the javelin. The other was for running hurdles. She was also a basketball and golf star.

The Lone Star State has also shone brightly on the baseball diamond. **Tris Speaker** (1888-1958) was born in Hubbard. He holds the career record for doubles with 793. **Rogers Hornsby** (1896-1963) was born in Winters. In 1924, Hornsby's batting average was .424. That's the highest average in modern baseball history.

Frank Robinson was born in Beaumont in 1935. Robinson belted 586 lifetime homers. He is fourth on the all-time list of home-run hitters. Home-run sluggers **Ernie Banks** and **Eddie Mathews** were born in Texas in 1931. Banks was born in Dallas. Mathews was born in Texarkana. Both men hit 512 homers.

The amazing pitcher **Nolan Ryan** was born

Athlete Babe Didrikson Zaharias

Pitcher Nolan Ryan

Jockey Willie Shoemaker

in Refugio in 1947. During his long career, he struck out 5,714 batters and pitched seven no-hitters. He retired from baseball in 1993.

Birthplace of Nolan Ryan, Barbara Jordan, Lyndon B. Johnson, and Babe Didrikson Zaharias...

Home to Stephen Austin, Sam Houston, Elisabet Ney, and George Bush...

The second-largest state, and the leading state for producing oil, beef cattle, horses, and cotton...

Site of the Alamo, the Astrodome, and the Johnson Space Center...

This is Texas—the Lone Star State!

Did You Know?

Marks called brands are placed on cattle to show who owns them. Texan Samuel Maverick did not brand his cattle herd. These cattle became known as "mavericks." Today, people who do not go along with the usual way of doing things are called "mavericks." Fans helped pick the name Mavericks for the Dallas pro basketball team.

Bracken Cave near San Antonio has one of the world's largest bat colonies. At times, there are twenty million of these flying animals in the cave.

Texas has many towns with unusual names. Trickham, Texas, was first called Trick 'Em. One of its storekeepers tricked his customers. There is a town named West in East Texas. The state also has towns named Happy, Oatmeal, Gun Barrel City, Sundown, Panhandle, Sugar Land, Lone Star, Cactus, Earth, and Buffalo. There used to be a community called Ding Dong in Bell County.

Americans have Mexican general Santa Anna to thank for chewing gum. In 1867, Santa Anna was in New York City. Americans saw him chewing something he didn't swallow. Santa Anna explained that he was chewing a substance that came from trees. A few years later, Americans began producing chewing gum in factories.

Heart surgeon Denton Cooley played in an orchestra made up only of doctors. They called themselves the "Heart Beats."

H. Ross Perot, Jr., and Jay Corburn of Dallas made the first around-the-world helicopter flight. They did this in the *Spirit of Texas* in September 1982.

In the late 1800s, a third of all Texas cowboys were of black or Mexican heritage.

In 1986, Roy Whetsline of Longview, Texas, paid ten dollars to buy a rock that looked like a potato. It proved to be a star sapphire worth over $2 million.

Elizabeth Watson was made Houston police chief in 1990. She became the nation's first woman to head a big city's police force.

Gene Autry's "Rudolph the Red-Nosed Reindeer" recording sold over fifty million copies.

A girl born in Beaumont in 1984 set the record for the longest name on a birth certificate. She was named Rhoshandiatellyneshia-unneveshenk Koyaanisquatsiuty Williams. A short time later, her first name was lengthened to 1,019 letters.

The Dallas Cowboys won the Super Bowl in 1972, 1978, 1993, and 1994.

Many famous Texans were once teachers. Sam Houston and William Travis both taught school before moving to Texas and becoming heroes. Lyndon B. Johnson taught at a Houston high school before becoming president. Mary Martin ran a dancing school before winning fame as an actress and singer. Texas governor Ann Richards recalls her years as a junior high-school teacher as "the hardest work I have done."

Dallas secretary Bette Nesmith Graham invented a white liquid to cover her typing errors. At first, it was called Mistake Out. Now called Liquid Paper, it is used by millions of people to correct typing mistakes.

Texas Information

State flag

Mockingbird

Chili

Area: 266,807 square miles (the second-largest state)

Greatest Distance North to South: 737 miles

Greatest Distance East to West: 774 miles

Borders: Arkansas and Louisiana to the east; Oklahoma to the north; New Mexico to the west; Mexico to the south and southwest; the Gulf of Mexico to the southeast

Highest Point: Guadalupe Peak, 8,751 feet above sea level

Lowest Point: Sea level, along the Gulf of Mexico

Hottest Recorded Temperature: 120° F. (at Seymour, on August 12, 1936)

Coldest Recorded Temperature: -23° F. (at Tulia, on February 12, 1899, then again at Seminole, on February 8, 1933)

Statehood: The twenty-eighth state, on December 29, 1845

Origin of Name: *Texas* comes from the Caddo Indian word *tejas,* meaning "friends"

Capital: Austin

Counties: 254 (the most counties of any state)

United States Senators: 2

United States Representatives: 30 (as of 1992)

State Senators: 31

State Representatives: 150

State Song: "Texas, Our Texas," by Gladys Yoakum Wright and William J. Marsh

State Motto: "Friendship"

Nickname: "Lone Star State"

State Seal: Front side adopted in 1845; reverse side adopted in 1961

State Flag: Adopted in 1839

State Flower: Bluebonnet

State Bird: Mockingbird

State Tree: Pecan

State Food: Chili

State Grass: Sideoats grama

State Fish: Guadalupe bass

State Gem: Texas blue topaz

State Stone: Petrified palmwood

State Shell: Lightning whelk

Some Rivers: Rio Grande, Red, Pecos, Brazos, Colorado, Sabine, Trinity, Guadalupe, Neches, Canadian

Some Islands: Galveston, Padre, Matagorda, Mustang

Some Mountain Ranges: Guadalupe, Davis, Santiago, Chisos

Wildlife: Deer, pronghorn antelopes, bobcats, mountain lions, coyotes, armadillos, beavers, opossums, foxes, bats, raccoons, alligators, rattlesnakes and many other kinds of snakes, mockingbirds, ducks, geese, cranes, roadrunners, many other kinds of birds

Manufactured Products: Chemicals, meats and many other kinds of foods, oil refining, plastics, airplanes, instruments, paints, clothing, computers and other kinds of machinery, ships and boats, toys, sporting goods

Farm Products: Beef cattle, horses, sheep, hogs, goats, turkeys, chickens, cotton, watermelons, rice, peanuts, pecans, hay, grapefruit, cucumbers, oranges, milk, sugar beets, tomatoes, lettuce, honey

Mining Products: Oil, natural gas, helium, uranium, limestone

Fishing Products: Shrimp, crabs, oysters, red snapper, trout, drum, flounder

Population: 16,986,510, third among the states (1990 U.S. Census Bureau figures)

Major Cities (1990 Census):

Houston	1,630,553	Fort Worth	447,619
Dallas	1,006,877	Arlington	261,721
San Antonio	935,933	Corpus Christi	257,453
El Paso	515,342	Lubbock	186,206
Austin	465,622		

Bluebonnets (with Indian paintbrush)

Pecan tree

Armadillo

57

Texas History

10,000 B.C.—The first people arrive in Texas

A.D. 1519—Spaniard Alonso Álvarez de Piñeda makes the first known exploration of Texas

1528—A Spanish vessel is wrecked along the Texas coast; four survivors then travel through Texas for a few years

1541—Spaniard Francisco de Coronado passes through Texas

1682—The first two Spanish missions are built in Texas

1685—Frenchman René-Robert Cavelier, Sieur de La Salle, founds a colony along the Gulf Coast

1718—The mission that is now known as the Alamo is founded

1772—San Antonio becomes the center of Spanish government in Texas

1776—The United States declares its independence from England

1813—Texas's first newspaper, *Gaceta de Texas (The Texas Gazette),* is printed at Nacogdoches

1820—Moses Austin plans an American colony in Texas

1821—Mexico gains its freedom from Spain and takes control of Texas; Stephen Austin brings the first American settlers to Texas

1835—The war for Texas's independence begins

1836—Texas declares its independence from Mexico; the Alamo falls; Sam Houston and his forces win the Battle of San Jacinto; Texas wins its independence from Mexico; Sam Houston is elected president of the Republic of Texas

1845—On December 29, Texas becomes the twenty-eighth state

1861—Texas leaves the Union and joins the Confederacy

1861-65—About 50,000 Texans serve in the Confederate army during the Civil War

1865—The last Civil War battle is fought at Palmito Hill

1866—Big cattle drives are started; oil is discovered

Sculptures of Alamo heroes William Travis and Davy Crockett are part of San Antonio's Alamo Monument.

1870—Texas is readmitted to the Union

1883—The University of Texas opens in Austin

1888—The state capitol is completed in Austin

1900—A hurricane kills at least 6,000 in the Galveston area

1901—The oil boom begins with a big discovery at Spindletop Hill near Beaumont

1917-18—After the United States enters World War I, more than 200,000 Texans serve

1925—Miriam A. "Ma" Ferguson becomes the first woman governor of Texas

1929-39—The Great Depression causes hard times in Texas

1941-45—After the United States enters World War II, 750,000 Texans serve

1947—About 510 people die when a ship explodes in the Texas City Harbor

1953—Dwight D. Eisenhower becomes the thirty-fourth president

1963—President John F. Kennedy is assassinated in Dallas on November 22; Lyndon B. Johnson then becomes the thirty-sixth president

1964—The Manned Spacecraft Center (later called the Johnson Space Center) opens in Houston

1972—Houston-born Barbara Jordan becomes the first black southern woman to be elected to the U.S. House of Representatives

1979—On April 10, tornadoes kill forty-two people in Wichita Falls and eleven in Vernon

1989—George Bush, a former Texas congressman, becomes the forty-first president

1990—The population of Texas reaches 16,986,510

1993—Kay Hutchison becomes Texas's first woman senator; a standoff between federal authorities and members of the Branch Davidian religious cult near Waco results in 79 deaths

1995—A new Mission Control facility opens in July at the Johnson Space Center in Houston

The Lyndon B. Johnson home in Johnson City

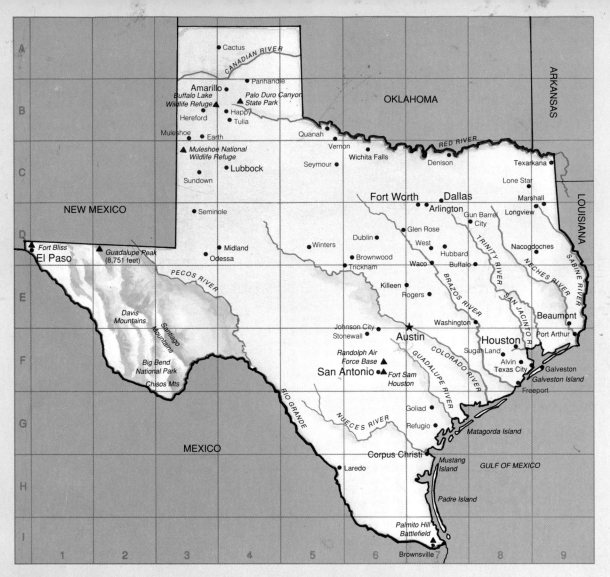

MAP KEY

Alvin	F8	Earth	B3	Lubbock	C4
Amarillo	B4	El Paso	D1	Marshall	D9
Arlington	D7	Fort Bliss	D1	Matagorda Island	G8
Austin	F7	Fort Sam Houston	F6	Midland	D4
Beaumont	E9	Fort Worth	C7	Muleshoe	B3
Big Bend National		Freeport	F8	Muleshoe National	
Park	F2,3	Galveston	F9	Wildlife Refuge	C3
Brazos River	E7	Galveston Island	F9	Mustang Island	H7
Brownsville	I7	Glen Rose	D7	Nacogdoches	D9
Brownwood	D6	Goliad	G7	Neches River	E8,9
Buffalo	E8	Guadalupe Peak	D2	Nueces River	G5,6
Buffalo Lake National		Guadalupe River	F,G7	Odessa	D3
Wildlife Refuge	B3	Gulf of Mexico	H8,9	Padre Island	H7
Cactus	A4	Gun Barrel City	D8	Palmito Hill	
Canadian River	A4	Happy	B4	Battlefield	I7
Chisos Mountains	F3	Hereford	B3	Palo Duro Canyon	
Colorado River	F7,8	Houston	F8	State Park	B4
Corpus Christi	H7	Hubbard	D7	Panhandle	B4
Dallas	C7	Johnson City	E6	Pecos River	E3
Davis Mountains	E2	Killeen	E6	Port Arthur	F9
Denison	C7	Laredo	H5	Quanah	B5
Dublin	D6	Lone Star	C8	Randolph A.F.B.	F6
		Longview	D9	Red River	C7

Refugio	G7
Rio Grande	G5
Rogers	E7
Sabine River	D,E9
San Antonio	F6
San Jacinto River	E,F8
Santiago Mountains	F3
Seminole	D3
Seymour	C5
Stonewall	F6
Sugar Land	F8
Sundown	C3
Texarkana	C9
Texas City	F8
Trickham	E6
Trinity River	D,E8
Tulia	B4
Vernon	C5
Waco	E7
Washington	E8
West	D7
Wichita Falls	C6
Winters	D5

GLOSSARY

annex: To add land to a country

artificial: Made by people rather than occurring naturally

assassinate: To murder someone who is in politics or government, usually by a secret or sudden attack

canyon: A deep, steep-sided valley

capital: The city that is the seat of government

capitol: The building in which the government meets

civil rights: The rights of a citizen

climate: The typical weather of a region

coast: The land along a large body of water

colony: A settlement that is outside a parent country and that is ruled by the parent country

crater: A pit in the ground made by an object such as a meteorite

drought: A period when rainfall is well below normal in an area

emancipation: The act of freeing people from slavery or from another form of control

explorer: A person who visits and studies unknown lands

hurdles: A race in which the runners must leap over obstacles

hurricane: A huge storm that forms over an ocean and that causes great damage when it reaches land

illiteracy: The inability to read and write

independence: Freedom from the control of others

integrate: To bring different races of people, such as black people and white people, together in the same schools, neighborhoods, and jobs

javelin: A light spear thrown for distance at track meets

meteorite: A piece of stone or metal from space that sometimes leaves a large hole when it strikes the ground

million: A thousand thousand (1,000,000)

mission: A settlement built around a church

monument: A building or statue that honors a person or famous event

petroleum: A scientific name for oil

pioneer: A person who is among the first to move into a region

pollute: To make dirty

population: The number of people in a place

port: A place along a coast where ships safely load and unload cargo

ragtime: A lively kind of music that was one of the roots of jazz music

rebel: A person who fights against his or her government

rodeo: An event at which cowboys and cowgirls show their skills

slave: A person who is owned by another person

surgeon: A doctor who performs operations

tornado: A powerful windstorm that comes from a whirling, funnel-shaped cloud and that causes great damage

PICTURE ACKNOWLEDGMENTS

Front Cover, © Tom Dietrich; 1, © Tom Till/Photographer; 2, Tom Dunnington; 3, © Walter Frerck/Odyssey Productions; 4-5, Tom Dunnington; 6-7, © Willard Clay/Dembinsky Photo Assoc.; 8, © Willard Clay/Dembinsky Photo Assoc.; 9 (left), © D. Muench/H. Armstrong Roberts; 9 (right), courtesy of Hammond, Incorporated, Maplewood, New Jersey; 10, © Tom Till/Photographer; 11, © Willard Clay/Dembinsky Photo Assoc.; 12, © Tom Till/Photographer; 13, George Nelson, artist, © University of Texas, The Institute of Texan Cultures, San Antonio, Texas; 14, The Institute of Texan Cultures, San Antonio, Texas; 15, © SuperStock; 16, Historical Pictures/Stock Montage; 17 (top), Historical Pictures/Stock Montage; 17 (bottom), © Photri; 18, Archives Division, Texas State Library; 19 (top), Historical Pictures/Stock Montage; 19 (bottom), Krause Publications, Inc., 700 E. State St., Iola, WI, 54990; 20, Austin History Center, Austin Public Library; 21, © Buddy Mays/Travel Stock; 22, The Erwin E. Smith Collection of the Library of Congress, on deposit at the Amon Carter Museum; 23, Archives Division, Texas State Library; 24, AP/Wide World Photos; 25, © Bob Glander/SuperStock; 27, AP/Wide World Photos; 28, © Buddy Mays/Travel Stock; 29 (top), © Joan Dunlop; 29 (bottom), © Robert E. Daemmrich/Tony Stone Worldwide/Chicago Ltd.; 30, © Buddy Mays/Travel Stock; 31 (top), © Walter Frerck/Odyssey Productions; 31 (bottom), © Buddy Mays/Travel Stock; 32-33, © George Hunter/H. Armstrong Roberts; 34, © Walter Frerck/Odyssey Productions; 35, © Willard Clay/Dembinsky Photo Assoc.; 36, © Tom Till/Photographer; 37 (top), © Photri; 37 (bottom), © Willard Clay/Dembinsky Photo Assoc.; 38 (both pictures), © Gene Ahrens; 39, © Robert E. Daemmrich/Tony Stone Worldwide/Chicago Ltd.; 40, © Buddy Mays/Travel Stock; 41 (top), © Peter Poulides/Tony Stone Worldwide/Chicago Ltd.; 41 (bottom), © Camerique/H. Armstrong Roberts; 42 (both pictures), © Joan Dunlop; 43, © Camerique/H. Armstrong Roberts; 44, AP/Wide World Photos; 45, © Gary Taylor/Tony Stone Worldwide/Chicago Ltd.; 46, courtesy of the West Point Museum Collection, U.S. Military Academy, West Point, NY; 47, Archives Division, Texas State Library; 48, Lyndon Baines Johnson Library, Austin, Art Kowart, photographer; 49 (both pictures), AP/Wide World Photos; 50 (both pictures), AP/Wide World Photos; 51 (top), UPI/Bettmann; 51 (bottom), AP/Wide World Photos; 52 (top), UPI/Bettmann; 52 (bottom), AP/Wide World Photos; 53, © Wide World Photos, Inc.; 54, © Merlin D. Tuttle, Bat Conservation International; 55, Denver Public Library, Western History Department; 56 (top), courtesy of Flag Research Center, Winchester, Massachusetts 01890; 56 (middle and bottom), © Buddy Mays/Travel Stock; 57 (top), © Doug Sherman/Geofile/Root Resources; 57 (middle), © Kohout Productions/Root Resources; 57 (bottom), © Camerique/H. Armstrong Roberts; 58, © Robert Frerck/Odyssey Productions; 59, © Robert E. Daemmrich/Tony Stone Worldwide/Chicago Ltd.; 60, Tom Dunnington; back cover, © Willard Clay/Dembinsky Photo Assoc.

INDEX

Page numbers in boldface type indicate illustrations.

ABOUT THE AUTHOR

Dennis Brindell Fradin is the author of 150 published children's books. His works for Childrens Press include the Young People's Stories of Our States series, the Disaster! series, and the Thirteen Colonies series. Dennis is married to Judith Bloom Fradin, who taught high-school and college English for many years. She is now Dennis's chief researcher. The Fradins are the parents of two sons, Anthony and Michael, and a daughter, Diana. Dennis graduated from Northwestern University in 1967 with a B.A. in creative writing, and has lived in Evanston, Illinois, since that year.